A List of Things I've Lost

TIFFANY BABB

Babb, Tiffany.
A List of Things I've Lost
First Edition. December, 2021

Library of Congress Control Number: 2021950996

ISBN: 978-1-952055-33-1

Cover art by Tiffany Babb

A List of Things I've Lost ©2021 **by** Tiffany Babb. Published in the United States by Vegetarian Alcoholic Poetry. Not one part of this work may be reproduced without expressed written consent from the author. For more information, please write V.A. Poetry, 643 South 2nd Street, Milwaukee, WI 53204

7 Each season steals a part of me away
8 The favored remnant of summer
9 Growing up
10 The forest in the lake
11 Midnight
12 Molten
13 On the Denali star
14 A brief memory
15 Persephone
16 Wake
17 Pressed memory
18 The simple prayer
19 Roost
20 Distance
21 In my dream, I was in love
22 November
23 Ships Lost off Howth
24 A List of things I've lost,
    or: How to adjust to a life without a father
25 Christina's world
26 Slow cacophony
27 Breaking the lease
28 Transformation
29 Night turn

30 Crows
31 Apparition
32 Prelude
33 On the upper Rhine, 1820
34 The middle part
35 Iced coffee
36 Before dawn
37 Distrust
38 Cathedral
39 The impossibility of imagining spring
40 All before it
41 September/October
42 At dawn
43 Living memory
44 Sunday theophany
45 Twenty-three
46 Edinburgh
47 Return
48 Tranquility
49 Seven years later
50 Visit
52 Thaw
53 Requiem
54 Slow recovery
55 Torrent
56 Fingerprints
57 After one hundred days of filtered air

for William H. Babb

Each season steals a part of me away

There might be   something left
of me   somewhere;
           here.

The streets, at least, remain
familiar.
                I retread
the path I took
as a child.

The favored remnant of summer

The smell of concrete dampened
by a hose, dust sloughing
off its surface, running
through the cracks.
Tiny rivulets
cause changes so small
you'd never notice
unless your cheek was pressed
up against the sidewalk,
your ear against
the grass.

Growing up

I cannot count the summers spent
nursing the few moments of freedom from school,
sitting on prickly grass, picking at weeds,
the gnarled bark of a pomegranate tree.

Above me, birds swirl, trying to mimic
the weightlessness of the clouds,
though I give them no notice.

Instead, I long for a friend,
certain that I will be alone forever.

As the sunlight fades and shadows grow long,
I place my hands on my head and watch
my silhouette transform into a large, unblinking eye.

The forest in the lake

      To run among the trees,
to see the sky   fractured
through their branches,
    bare feet firm
    on glassy water.

    I could find peace
from the gnawing feeling.

                Free

to revel in
aloneness,
to race after
      danger,

and then
    to find someone
to share this mirror
to another world.

Midnight

Summer heat refuses to give in
to the expectations of night.

Under flickering streetlamps,
bugs gather in glittering clouds.

Cockroaches scuttle
across still-warm sidewalks
careful to avoid encroaching
footsteps.

In the gutter, molten gold
runs into black.

I wonder if this
feeling lasts.

Molten

At six, I caught the end
of a news report
—volcanoes on Mars.

The idea thrilled me,
filled me to the brim
with dreams of space.

I saw myself
scuffing sneakers
with copper dirt,
as I searched
for a way home.

That night, I woke
with nightmares of lava
pouring down to earth
like rain.

On the Denali star

      Paying too close attention
to the uncertainty
      blooming,

      I miss the changing of seasons,
      the conjuring
of yellow-green leaves,

tufts of grass poking through
warm soil.

A brief memory

Before returning home,
I duck into Central Park
to savor a rare hour of temperate weather.

The trees loom like fat nurses
towering over their charges.
Heavy arms sprinkling pollen
over the path.

You used to sneeze in the spring.

Persephone

I think back to home,
where the sun was too bright,
and every day was a warning.
How many times was I told
to be careful where I walked?

I slip pomegranate seeds
into my mouth, wait
until the world is watching,
and bite down.

In an instant,
the world turns,
and the sky is beneath
my feet.

Above me, the ground closes in.
The cool darkness, a relief.
I feel each shovelful of dirt
as it settles against my skin
even before I can taste—

I think back to home.
As I rise, I am overcome
by the blinding light
of a brilliant, red sun.

Wake

At a certain point there is little to do
but turn out the lights and retreat to bed.
The darkness is kinder than her sister. Always eager
to engulf everything, never asking
for anything we cannot give.

Pressed memory

Vines thread through the chain link fence,
a scatter of dagger-sharp leaves.

I pluck one, press it in a book,
hope that I can save that shade of green,
the end of summer.

The simple prayer

Dirty dishes wait
in the empty kitchen.

Outside,
blades of grass
dip under the weight
of dew,

a humble offering to
the silent hours

Roost

A cloud of blackbirds
perches on the crooked tree,
They launch into the air, hover,
before landing once more.
I watch them late into the evening,
trying to understand the thought
behind their near constant movement.
It isn't until the sky darkens
that I leave them to their folly,
and they leave me to mine.

Distance

The wind whips at our faces
while we pass around a cigarette
on the brink of extinguishing.

The hood of the car is still warm.
We sit on it and pretend the thermos isn't empty
and that the cold isn't already unbearable.

When we tilt our heads back,
we can't see the stars.

Tonight exists between now
and tomorrow, and we are afraid
of tomorrow.

In my Dream, I was in love

We walked on a seaside cliff,
watching the seagulls thread
through the clouds until it was time
for us to jump into breaking waves.

November

The first of November is marked
by the unearthing of last winter's
wardrobe.

Dusty coats, cheap gloves—
temporary replacements
for the ones   you lost
years ago.

And a scarf,   newly knitted,
in cream-colored yarn.

You duck behind it
like a turtle who retreats into the shell
she claims will protect her.

Ships Lost off Howth

It takes time for our eyes to adjust
to the cramped room lit by amber lamps
and an old fireplace in the corner.
Old men sit in circles, drinking beer,
and trading off from gossiping
to grabbing guitars and singing.

As I wait, I read the words
carefully painted on the wall.
Ships Lost off Howth. Below,
a list of names like The Flying Dart,
Roxane, along with the year
each ship was lost.

I wonder who put the names together,
copying each date in crooked script.
I remember that it takes work to remember,
and that I have failed again and again to take part
in the ritual of it, pressing my palms into the sand,
knowing the tide will free my attempts into
swirling clouds beneath the water.

A list of things I've lost,
or: how to adjust to a life without a father

Faster than I can keep note,
the tiny enamel pins
that adorn my bag fall,
one by one,
leaving behind only
rubber backings that gather
alongside gum wrappers
and receipts.

Pencils – expensive ones,
slip out of my hair,
my pockets, along
with tiny candy-colored
notebooks, half filled
with to-do lists
and contact information.

There is a permanency to lost things,
and I track each moment
I had a thing last, determine
what I might have done
to spare its fate.

Christina's world
After Andrew Wyeth

The dew soaks into her skin,
has already soaked
        into her dress.

        Far away,
        a house is filled with things
        that need doing.

It disappears
when she turns
to look at the sky.

Slow cacophony

The click of spoons against a plate,
the whir of the range hood,
something sizzling in a pan.

Was it ever quiet in this house?
Half-remembered sounds come to haunt me.
Echoes of a life that has not been for years.

I leave the first chance I get,
climb into the car and drive,
looking for somewhere familiar
to stop.

Breaking the lease

The keys clink as they slide down
the sides of the manila envelope.

I check that everything is in place
and then seal it, grabbing hold
of the accompanying slip of paper.

        I always keep receipts,
too nervous about throwing away anything
important to trust the permanence
of a garbage can.

They accumulate
in glove compartments,
jacket pockets, and at the corners
of tote bags, until the print fades
and the paper grows
crisp and yellow.

Transformation

At noon,
        dreams grow
sour   alongside the scent
of your breath   and moldering
orange peels.

Peering through the curtains, my mother
remarks that the weather is about to turn.

Turn into what?

Night turn

From the grey
overwhelming
sense
      nausea

pain

                clarity
and the quiet
that turns a whisper
to thunder
to nothingness again

Crows

The old ones know better
than to rouse at dawn
and squabble over sleepy worms.
Food will appear or it won't.

There will always be a day
when one goes hungry,
when the worms fail to appear,
the sun sets, and we all fall silent.

Apparition

Under the light of half-gone candles,
our insecurities unwrap.
The false warmth of a hand
wrapping around my own,
breath brushing against neck.
In another room, a lamp flickers.

Prelude

Throughout the week,
a layer of fog hovers
above the apartment building.
At night, it catches the orange glow
of the football field,
The trees, magnificent and bare,
thread dark cracks into the pale light.

On the upper Rhine, 1820
After J.M.W. Turner

Beneath the storm clouds,
the moon bobs in the river.

A logger's raft sways,
back and forth.

The path ahead,
is obscured by cliffs.

There is little to do
but push forward,
to find comfort in the distance
we put between us
and the past.

Ahead, nothing
but water and stone
and night sky.

The middle part

After two weeks away from home,
I return to where people are going
about their daily lives.

I have yet to settle,
sluggish from lack of sleep.
My luggage is still packed, half open
on the bedroom floor.

When the sun rises, I make my way
to the grocery store, picking up eggs, milk, an apple.

Life has become impossible to ignore.
Something boils beneath my skin.
I am overwhelmed with the urge to run.

Iced coffee

Melting ice chips rattle
against the walls of a plastic cup.
Behind us, high school students pluck
at out-of-tune guitars. Birds hop, leaving divots
in the loose gravel at our feet.

Plastic bottles click, and a gust of wind
launches dust into our eyes.
We blink the grit away and cry.

Before dawn

Our shadows meld
Our bodies seizing

from the inside   broken
breaking
          into pieces
that we can't see   or
put back

        into place.

We used to wonder how
we appeared,
sitting together   on a park bench

heads bowed
      underneath
streetlights   about to lose
power.

Distrust

Where are
our secrets held?   Sinking or secure
              in the heavy space,
              dark

red, wine sour, underneath our tongues,
leftover from yesterday

Now our words are echoes of what   we've forgotten,
our conversations ghost   apparitions from when we
were less afraid

Cathedral

Your eyes are stained glass
poised to shatter,

ready to fall apart into
sharp-edged jewels,

glinting against the cold
grey floor. Your body

remains sturdy—
weather beaten;

your hard edges turned
soft. Your feet, your legs,

your trunk and neck are stone
slabs reaching

towards the more perfect
planets. While I, too

clumsy, too heavy and marred
to ascend anywhere, tread

with my ankles sinking
into earth, rooted, rooting.

When the wind blows,
my edges do not soften,
I die.

The impossibility of imagining spring

We cannot show
the scars of our pasts
on our faces.

Instead, we choose
to not bear
      children.

Afraid, so afraid
      of losing time,
      of losing self,

      of facing the worst
that the world has to offer
a child,
to us.   Barren.

How to give
name to a   lack?

Unable to know, we overturn
frozen ground, reveal what
winter has hidden.

All before it
After Cy Twombly's The Fire that Consumes All Before It (1978)

Fire is always becoming
something it is not.   Acting,
as itself, upon others.
        A brutal means

of transformation from thing
to un-thing.   From orange to
un-orange.
           From yellow
to blue to white.

Fingers scrape through fat
mixed with ash, burnt
bits of paper.

September/October

Just as the sun appears,
it fades, and it is
dark again.

It's hard, to not let
the cold seep
into your head.

The list of unfinished
tasks grows.

Each day
your weariness
compounds.

Day has begun
to slip into night
unnoticed.

At dawn

We are left   emptier
than we remember
being.

We do not reach   for
each other as we   look
to the sky.

Broken, jagged, and bare,
we   straighten our backs,
steel ourselves
for the sunlight.

The realization that we are
expected
to move   forward from here
is a curse.

Living memory

How familiar it all is,
navigating sterile corridors,
watching the slow drip of an IV machine.

It takes only a day to learn
which nurse to ask for a spare pillow
and which one to avoid.

Even the flowers look the same,
arranged in plastic vases,
out of place in the sterile room.

It feels as if five years haven't passed,
as if we never really rested after the first time.
How quickly this life sucks you back in,
steals your sleep, steals the silence away.

The janitor who brings you coffee after a long night—
small gestures from strangers, that is familiar too.
But still, we have changed.
Now, we are quick to recognize the signs of death.
We know the cost of trying to heal
when there is no healing to be done.

Sunday theophany

Every Sunday morning,
I would sit, ramrod straight
and look up-up-up
to where Jesus stared down
from the vaulted ceiling.

He was terrifying, enormous,
encircled in golden flames,
glaring down with white, empty eyes
to where I sat.

He was always so expressionless,
as if he saw nothing there.

Twenty-three

I can see my grandmother at my age
pull her hands from family and home,
to flee from country to country to
country again, so that I might see
the Notre Dame, hear chatter
from the flower market
opening nearby.

In my bag, a pass for the Metro,
details for my flight home,
and a set of house keys,
jangling.

Edinburgh

In the fruit cart,
an unexpected gift,
peaches in late December.

This trip has been plagued
with nausea left over
from the long flight.

Still, I pick three pieces of fruit,
let them drop against the container
of shortbread at the bottom of my bag,
the promises of a picnic.

On Calton Hill, I sit alone
among half-built monuments.

The sun rises, melting frost into dew,
and I bite into a peach,
a million miles from home.

Return

The house is empty;
only the kitchen light is on.

Taped to the staircase is a note
from my grandmother on a scrap
torn from a wall calendar.

Characters march in neat little rows,
scratched out in skipping ballpoint ink.
I recognize only my name and the symbol for night.

I pass them to a friend who tells me
the scrawl is too messy to decipher.
Then to my mother next, who translates
as only a child can, for their parent,
with patience and familiarity.

The church meeting will run late.
There is food in the fridge.
Do not wait up to let me in.

Tranquility

At the dining table of a freezing kitchen
I sit alongside candles of pearled wax,
an empty napkin holder, last night's wine glass.

Here, the sun exists only in weak beams
slipping through the curtain of clouds.

Leftover rain drips from tree leaves, and
hydrangeas dash blue and purple through green.

Seven years later

In this light, the snow drift looks blue.
You've been gone for longer than you were here.
The house seems emptier when it's cold;
these are broken bones beyond repair.

You've been gone for longer than you were here.
—each year I see you less and less.
These are broken bones beyond repair;
even memory has begun to fail.

Each year I see you less and less,
and I look at my own face in the mirror.
Even memory has begun to fail.
I don't know what I'm looking for.

I look at my own face in the mirror.
The house seems emptier when it's cold.
I don't know what I'm looking for
—in this light, the snow drift looks blue.

Visit

Hospitals are all the same,
characterized by tense shoulders,
the call of machinery,
bright unwavering lights,
all radiating fear

      of the future, of what was said
or not said, done or not done.

I watch
a woman sat
across the waiting room,
collapsed on a faded cloth chair,
eating a sandwich.

I imagine how each bite tastes—
the bland cafeteria bread, the crunch
of soggy lettuce, slimy seeds
of tomato against threads
of dry turkey.

Her eyes drift towards the door,
expecting a doctor to come.
    It's torture,
that   wondering.
Though I would trade it
with the waiting
that I am doing now.

She finishes the sandwich,
sweeps away the crumbs.
I listen to the rustle
of the plastic wrapper.

Thaw

As if it never left, heat blooms
through the air, unfurling my fingertips with warmth.
I clench and unclench my fist, experiment
with the newfound sensations,   the ability
to wake up in the morning
 and not have to wait   to thaw.

                         Spring comes
as a surprise each year— we scramble
to rediscover   what we'd forgotten
during the days when we believed
the sun would not return.

Requiem

What haunts me is the sound,

the wind whispering above
the tall stalks of grass
where my grandparents hid
from the men who would kill
their families and everyone they knew.

I am afraid of the memories
—the ones which are not mine
but dictate my life.

Sitting at my desk, I falter,
frozen in that moment.

I am unsure of what to make
of myself.

Slow recovery

To reclaim use of our bodies,
we chew   stale toast and sip
tea.

It takes   time to gather
the energy   we lost,
toss   clothes
into hamper,
take the bag of trash
outside,

pack away the detritus
and open the window
to let the air in.

You sit back down, tired already,
and wait   as the smell
of smoke from the cigar shop
downstairs
drowns out the memories
of confinement
      and being still.

Torrent

Outside the Columbus Circle stop,
water begins to fall from the sky.

A blast of air, and the drizzle shifts to a torrent.
For a moment, everything freezes. Then, mass exodus—
to awnings, subway stations, coffee shop alcoves.

Those with umbrellas scramble for them,
lift fabric shields towards the sky.
Those who push forward without reprieve
meet eyes, laugh at the absurdity of the situation,
look up at the sky, down at soaked clothes,
and wipe water from bright smiling faces.

Fingerprints

We can't control everything
least of all   the ground that falls
away beneath our feet.

We are growing
older,
and running   out
of second chances.

What will we leave
behind
this time?   Fingerprints
on empty glasses, unmade   beds,
windows left   open,
all those
little things

I was too afraid   to ask
                for you

to return.

After one hundred days of filtered air

of food   carefully dried,
of seeing the same
faces, of the sun
through a plate of glass.

The world
inside is sterile,   each aspect controlled.

A single sprout reaching up,
green and wanting,
through the dirt   we brought
with us.

Outside is everything
we can't control.
Though we are   afraid,
we step out
of our suits   to face
       the storm.

Acknowledgements

"The favored remnants of summer" and "After one hundred days of filtered air" published in *Cardiff Review*

"Molten" published in *Graviton Lit*

"Tranquility" and "Sunday theophany" published in *Moon Mic*

"Persephone" published in *Anti-Heroin Chic*

"The impossibility of imagining spring" published in *Dunes Review*

"All Before It" published in *Rust+Moth*

"Edinburgh," "Roost," and "Crows" published in *Third Wednesday*

My deepest thanks to my mother and sister for their unwavering support throughout my writing life (and actual life too). Thanks to my grandmother for countless meals as I was growing up and to Evelyn Chang for bringing lattes on the worst day of my life. Love to my Tia Carol, who always reminds me so much of my dad. Much gratitude to Neil Aitken and Kanika Lawton for their early notes on this manuscript. My love to Emalyn Feitshans, Audrey Kwon, Bryn Dunbar, Allison Manuel, Madison Lewis, for being fellow writers in crime and for talking me off the perilous cliffs that always seem to appear when we muddle through writing. A friendly shoutout to the faculty and students of The New School Creative Writing Program. Grateful acknowledgments to Cardiff Review, Graviton Lit, Anti-Heroin Chic, Third Wednesday Magazine, Dunes Review, Rust+Moth, and Moon Mic, where some of these poems first appeared. Last but not least, thanks to Freddy La Force at Vegetarian Alcoholic Press for turning my plain manuscript into a beautiful and very real book.

www.ingramcontent.com/pod-product-compliance
Lightning Source LLC
Chambersburg PA
CBHW062035120526
44592CB00036B/2188